THIS JOURNAL BELONGS TO:

_____

Scripture taken from the NEW AMERICAN STANDARD BIBLE®,
Copyright © 1960,1962,1963,1968,1971,1972,1973,1975,1977,1995
by The Lockman Foundation. Used by permission.

Scriptures quoted from the International Children's Bible®,
copyright ©1986, 1988, 1999, 2015 by Tommy Nelson. Used by permission.

Scripture quotations are taken from the Holy Bible, New Living Translation,
copyright © 1996, 2004, 2015 by Tyndale House Foundation.
Used by permission of Tyndale House Publishers, Inc.,
Carol Stream, Illinois 60188. All rights reserved.

Printed in the United States of America
First Printing, 2019

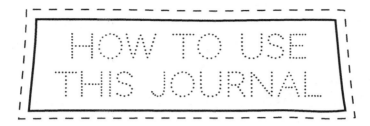
HOW TO USE
THIS JOURNAL

Get to know yourself
& your relationship with God better!

Take a few minutes each day to answer the
daily question and read the daily verse.

Have Fun and be free!

Each daily spread has a full page for you to write
down any to-do lists, doodle to your heart's content, or
to dream up a new goal or idea - don't hold back!

Think back
and get ready for a new week!

Every 7 days there is a weekly check-in where you
have space to reflect back on the week, consider how
you might do things differently in the future, write
down your prayers to God, and think about if any
prayers have been answered in your life.

WEEKLY CHECK-IN

What are the
3 best things that
happened to you
this week?

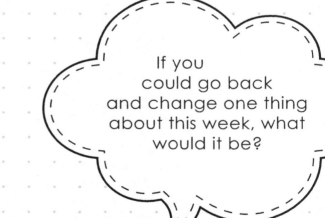

If you
could go back
and change one thing
about this week, what
would it be?

Write down things you need help with or are worried about. Use this list to help you pray to God each day. Add to this list if new concerns pop up during the week!

TODAYS DATE:

If you could ask God only one question and get an answer, what would you ask?

DAILY QUESTION

TO-DO'S, DOODLES, & DREAMS:

"Call to Me and I will answer you, and I will tell you great and mighty things, which you do not know."

JEREMIAH 33:3

TODAYS DATE:

What do you pretend to hate
but actually love?

DAILY QUESTION

TO-DO'S, DOODLES, & DREAMS:

And you will know the truth, and the truth will set you free.

JOHN 8:32

TODAYS DATE:

You have the exact same meal (breakfast, lunch and dinner) for the next 12 months. What do you pick and why?

DAILY QUESTION

TO-DO'S, DOODLES, & DREAMS:

So whether you eat or drink, or whatever you do,
do it all for the glory of God.

1 Corinthians 10:31

TODAYS DATE:

Do you think money
can buy happiness?

DAILY QUESTION

TO-DO'S, DOODLES, & DREAMS:

For the love of money is the root of all kinds of evil. And some people, craving money, have wandered from the true faith and pierced themselves with many sorrows.

1 TIMOTHY 6:10

TODAYS DATE:

When you feel down, do you prefer hugs or words of encouragement from your parents?

DAILY QUESTION

TO-DO'S, DOODLES, & DREAMS:

This is my command—be strong and courageous! Do not be afraid or discouraged. For the Lord your God is with you wherever you go.

JOSHUA 1:9

TODAYS DATE:

Do you believe in miracles? Do you think you have ever seen or known of one happening?

DAILY QUESTION

TO-DO'S, DOODLES, & DREAMS:

Jesus said to her, "I am the resurrection and the life; he who believes in Me will live even if he dies, and everyone who lives and believes in Me will never die. Do you believe this?"

JOHN 11:25-26

TODAYS DATE:

What's something you know you
do differently than most people?

DAILY QUESTION

TO-DO'S, DOODLES, & DREAMS:

Dear friends, let us continue to love one another, for love comes from God. Anyone who loves is a child of God and knows God.

1 JOHN 4:7

WEEKLY CHECK-IN

What are the
3 best things that
happened to you
this week?

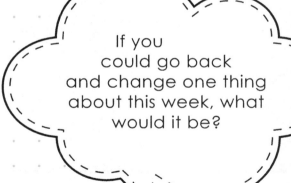

If you
could go back
and change one thing
about this week, what
would it be?

Write down things you need help with or are worried about. Use this list to help you pray to God each day. Add to this list if new concerns pop up during the week!

Think back on this last week - do you remember any prayers being answered or do you feel like God spoke to you in any way?

TODAYS DATE:

How often do you pray to God?

DAILY QUESTION

TO-DO'S, DOODLES, & DREAMS:

Always be happy. Never stop praying. Give thanks whatever happens. That is what God wants for you in Christ Jesus.

1 THESSALONIANS 5:16-18

TODAYS DATE:

You are an important person
to others! Who do you consider
the most important
person in your life?

DAILY QUESTION

TO-DO'S, DOODLES, & DREAMS:

For the Lord your God is living among you. He is a mighty savior. He will take delight in you with gladness. With his love, he will calm all your fears. He will rejoice over you with joyful songs.

ZEPHANIAH 3:17

TODAYS DATE:

Would you rather read a book or watch a movie?

DAILY QUESTION

TO-DO'S, DOODLES, & DREAMS:

For the Lord grants wisdom! From his mouth
come knowledge and understanding.

PROVERBS 2:6

TODAYS DATE:

Have you ever had to
apologize to someone?
Did that make you feel better
about a situation?

DAILY QUESTION

TO-DO'S, DOODLES, & DREAMS:

Whenever you stand praying, forgive, if you have anything
against anyone, so that your Father who is in heaven
will also forgive you your transgressions.

MARK 11:25

TODAYS DATE:

God made you in His image, so why is it that we sometimes feel down about how we look?

DAILY QUESTION

TO-DO'S, DOODLES, & DREAMS:

So God created human beings in his image. In the image of God he created them. He created them male and female.

GENESIS 1:27

TODAYS DATE:

How can you encourage
a friend who might
be feeling down?

DAILY QUESTION

TO-DO'S, DOODLES, & DREAMS:

Now may the God of hope fill you with all joy and peace in believing, so that you will abound in hope by the power of the Holy Spirit.

ROMANS 15:13

TODAYS DATE:

God loves you! How can you show God's love to others?

DAILY QUESTION

TO-DO'S, DOODLES, & DREAMS:

For God loved the world so much that he gave his only Son.
God gave his Son so that whoever believes in him
may not be lost, but have eternal life.

JOHN 3:16

WEEKLY CHECK-IN

Write down things you need help with or are worried about. Use this list to help you pray to God each day. Add to this list if new concerns pop up during the week!

Think back on this last week - do you remember any prayers being answered or do you feel like God spoke to you in any way?

What's your idea
of a perfect day?

DAILY QUESTION

TO-DO'S, DOODLES, & DREAMS:

But the Holy Spirit produces this kind of fruit in our lives: love, joy, peace, patience, kindness, goodness, faithfulness, gentleness, and self-control. There is no law against these things!

GALATIANS 5:22-23

TODAYS DATE:

If you could change
one thing about the world,
what would it be?

DAILY QUESTION

TO-DO'S, DOODLES, & DREAMS:

And this world is fading away, along with everything that people crave. But anyone who does what pleases God will live forever.

1 JOHN 2:17

TODAYS DATE:

The most creative solution to a problem I've ever used was...

TO-DO'S, DOODLES, & DREAMS:

All Scripture is inspired by God and is useful to teach us what is true and to make us realize what is wrong in our lives. It corrects us when we are wrong and teaches us to do what is right. God uses it to prepare and equip his people to do every good work.

2 TIMOTHY 3:16-17

TODAYS DATE:

What do you look forward to when you wake up?

DAILY QUESTION

TO-DO'S, DOODLES, & DREAMS:

The faithful love of the Lord never ends! His mercies never cease. Great is his faithfulness; his mercies begin afresh each morning.

LAMENTATIONS 3:22-23

TODAYS DATE:

What is the hardest thing you
have ever done?

DAILY QUESTION

TO-DO'S, DOODLES, & DREAMS:

So don't worry, because I am with you. Don't be afraid,
because I am your God. I will make you strong and will help you.
I will support you with my right hand that saves you.

ISAIAH 41:10

TODAYS DATE:

What's something you do so well that you could teach it to others?

DAILY QUESTION

TO-DO'S, DOODLES, & DREAMS:

God has given each of you a gift from his great variety
of spiritual gifts. Use them well to serve one another.

1 PETER 4:10

TODAYS DATE:

What would you say were the most important moments of your life so far?

DAILY QUESTION

TO-DO'S, DOODLES, & DREAMS:

And the Word became flesh, and dwelt among us, and we saw
His glory, glory as of the only begotten from the Father,
full of grace and truth.

JOHN 1:14

WEEKLY CHECK-IN

What are the
3 best things that
happened to you
this week?

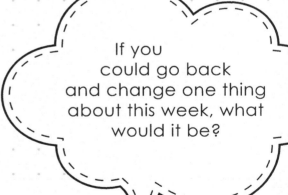

If you
could go back
and change one thing
about this week, what
would it be?

Write down things you need help with or are worried about. Use this list to help you pray to God each day. Add to this list if new concerns pop up during the week!

Think back on this last week - do you remember any prayers being answered or do you feel like God spoke to you in any way?

TODAYS DATE:

Why do you think people are critical of how others look? Do looks really matter?

DAILY QUESTION

TO-DO'S, DOODLES, & DREAMS:

Don't be concerned about the outward beauty of fancy hairstyles,
expensive jewelry, or beautiful clothes. You should clothe yourselves
instead with the beauty that comes from within, the unfading
beauty of a gentle and quiet spirit, which is so precious to God.

1 PETER 3:3-4

TODAYS DATE:

When you are sad,
what makes you happy?

DAILY QUESTION

TO-DO'S, DOODLES, & DREAMS:

Jesus said, "Don't let your hearts be troubled.
Trust in God. And trust in me."

JOHN 14:1

TODAYS DATE:

One thing I think God wants me
to share with others is...

DAILY QUESTION

TO-DO'S, DOODLES, & DREAMS:

Tell of His glory among the nations,
His wonderful deeds among all the peoples.

PSALM 96:3

If you were trying out for a singing contest reality show, what song would you sing?

TO-DO'S, DOODLES, & DREAMS:

Come, let us sing to the Lord!
Let us shout joyfully to the Rock of our salvation.

PSALM 95:1

TODAYS DATE:

Would you rather have $100 to keep for yourself or $1,000 to give to charity?

DAILY QUESTION

TO-DO'S, DOODLES, & DREAMS:

Being kind to the poor is like lending to the Lord.
The Lord will reward you for what you have done.

PROVERBS 19:17

TODAYS DATE:

Is there any place in the world you would like to visit?

DAILY QUESTION

TO-DO'S, DOODLES, & DREAMS:

We can make our plans, but the Lord determines our steps.

PROVERBS 16:9

What is the weirdest thing you have ever eaten?

TODAYS DATE:

DAILY QUESTION

TO-DO'S, DOODLES, & DREAMS:

Jesus replied,"I am the bread of life.
Whoever comes to me will never be hungry again.
Whoever believes in me will never be thirsty."

JOHN 6:35

WEEKLY CHECK-IN

Write down things you need help with or are worried about. Use this list to help you pray to God each day. Add to this list if new concerns pop up during the week!

Think back on this last week - do you remember any prayers being answered or do you feel like God spoke to you in any way?

TODAYS DATE:

Describe yourself in 5 words.

DAILY QUESTION

TO-DO'S, DOODLES, & DREAMS:

And I will be your Father, and you will be
my sons and daughters, says the Lord Almighty.

2 CORINTHIANS 6:18

Would you rather be really talented at one thing, or be good at lots of things?

DAILY QUESTION

TO-DO'S, DOODLES, & DREAMS:

Everything you say and everything you do should all be done for Jesus your Lord. And in all you do, give thanks to God the Father through Jesus.

COLOSSIANS 3:17

TODAYS DATE:

If you could only listen to one song for the rest of your life, which song would you pick?

DAILY QUESTION

TO-DO'S, DOODLES, & DREAMS:

Sing to him; yes, sing his praises.
Tell everyone about his wonderful deeds.

PSALM 105:2

TODAYS DATE:

If you had to choose one,
would you rather be invisible
or be able to fly?

DAILY QUESTION

TO-DO'S, DOODLES, & DREAMS:

*Now may the God of hope fill you with all joy
and peace in believing, so that you will abound in hope
by the power of the Holy Spirit.*

ROMANS 15:13

TODAYS DATE:

If you formed a League
of Not-So-Super Heroes and
chose five members with lame
super powers... who are they and
what are their powers?

DAILY QUESTION

TO-DO'S, DOODLES, & DREAMS:

God' power protects you through your faith,
and it keeps you safe until your salvation comes.
That salvation is ready to be
given to you at the end of time.

1 PETER 1:5

How do you think someone becomes a Christian?

TODAYS DATE:

DAILY QUESTION

TO-DO'S, DOODLES, & DREAMS:

If you openly declare that Jesus is Lord and believe in your heart that God raised him from the dead, you will be saved.

ROMANS 10:9

TODAYS DATE:

What makes a house
an actual home?

DAILY QUESTION

TO-DOS, DOODLES, & DREAMS:

Jesus said,"Don't let your hearts be troubled. Trust in God.
And trust in me. There are many rooms in my Father's house.
I would not tell you this if it were not true.
I am going there to prepare a place for you."

JOHN 14:1-2

WEEKLY CHECK-IN

What are the
3 best things that
happened to you
this week?

If you
could go back
and change one thing
about this week, what
would it be?

Write down things you need help with or are worried about. Use this list to help you pray to God each day. Add to this list if new concerns pop up during the week!

Think back on this last week - do you remember any prayers being answered or do you feel like God spoke to you in any way?

What thing does not exist that someone needs to invent?

DAILY QUESTION

TO-DO'S, DOODLES, & DREAMS:

Jesus looked at them intently and said,
"Humanly speaking, it is impossible. But not with God.
Everything is possible with God."

MARK 10:27

TODAYS DATE:

If you could make up a rule that everyone in your family had to follow, what would it be?

DAILY QUESTION

TO-DO'S, DOODLES, & DREAMS:

"Children, obey your parents because you belong to the Lord,
for this is the right thing to do. "Honor your father and mother."
This is the first commandment with a promise:
If you honor your father and mother, "things will go well for you,
and you will have a long life on the earth."

EPHESIANS 6:1-3

My life would be better if...

DAILY QUESTION

TO-DO'S, DOODLES, & DREAMS:

You can make many plans, but the Lord's purpose will prevail.

PROVERBS 19:21

TODAYS DATE:

If you could change your name,
what would you change it to?

DAILY QUESTION

TO-DO'S, DOODLES, & DREAMS:

For a child will be born to us, a son will be given to us; And the government will rest on His shoulders; And His name will be called Wonderful Counselor, Mighty God, Eternal Father, Prince of Peace.

ISAIAH 9:6

TODAYS DATE:

What is the one thing you have learned in life that you think you will use often as an adult?

DAILY QUESTION

TO-DOS, DOODLES, & DREAMS:

If you need wisdom, ask our generous God,
and he will give it to you. He will not rebuke you for asking.

JAMES 1:5

TODAYS DATE:

Which is worse,
failing or never trying?

DAILY QUESTION

TO-DO'S, DOODLES, & DREAMS:

We can rejoice, too, when we run into problems and trials, for
we know that they help us develop endurance. And endurance
develops strength of character, and character strengthens
our confident hope of salvation. And this hope will not lead to
disappointment. For we know how dearly God loves us, because he
has given us the Holy Spirit to fill our hearts with his love.

ROMANS 5:3-5

TODAYS DATE:

What brings you comfort?

DAILY QUESTION

TO-DOS, DOODLES, & DREAMS:

Even when I walk through the darkest valley, I will not be afraid, for you are close beside me. Your rod and your staff protect and comfort me.

PSALM 23:4

WEEKLY CHECK-IN

What are the
3 best things that
happened to you
this week?

If you
could go back
and change one thing
about this week, what
would it be?

Write down things you need help with or are worried about. Use this list to help you pray to God each day. Add to this list if new concerns pop up during the week!

Think back on this last week - do you remember any prayers being answered or do you feel like God spoke to you in any way?

TODAYS DATE:

What is your favorite word?

DAILY QUESTION

TO-DO'S, DOODLES, & DREAMS:

Wise words satisfy like a good meal;
the right words bring satisfaction.

PROVERBS 18:20

TODAYS DATE:

Is there something that you are afraid to pray for?

DAILY QUESTION

TO-DO'S, DOODLES, & DREAMS:

Trust in the Lord with all your heart;
do not depend on your own understanding.
Seek his will in all you do, and he will
show you which path to take.

PROVERBS 3:5-6

TODAYS DATE:

If you could ask Christ to change one problem in the world today, what would you like him to change?

DAILY QUESTION

TO-DOS, DOODLES, & DREAMS:

Then Jesus again spoke to them, saying,
"I am the Light of the world; he who follows Me
will not walk in the darkness, but will have the Light of life."

JOHN 8:12

TODAYS DATE:

How would you describe the word "Love" without using that word?

DAILY QUESTION

TO-DO'S, DOODLES, & DREAMS:

Love is patient and kind. Love is not jealous, it does not brag, and
it is not proud. Love is not rude, is not selfish, and does not become
angry easily. Love does not remember wrongs done against it.
Love takes no pleasure in evil, but rejoices over the truth.
Love patiently accepts all things. It always trusts, always
hopes, and always continues strong.

1 CORINTHIANS 13:4-7

TODAYS DATE:

Besides your parents, do you
have a favorite family member?

DAILY QUESTION

TO-DOS, DOODLES, & DREAMS:

*Anyone who does the will of my Father in heaven
is my brother and sister and mother!*

MATTHEW 12:50

TODAYS DATE:

Do you have any bad habits?

DAILY QUESTION

TO-DO'S, DOODLES, & DREAMS:

The temptations in your life are no different from what others experience. And God is faithful. He will not allow the temptation to be more than you can stand. When you are tempted, he will show you a way out so that you can endure.

1 CORINTHIANS 10:13

If you were a crayon color, what color would you be?

TODAYS DATE:

DAILY QUESTION

TO-DO'S, DOODLES, & DREAMS:

I have placed my rainbow in the clouds.
It is the sign of my covenant with you and with all the earth.

GENESIS 9:13

WEEKLY CHECK-IN

What are the
3 best things that
happened to you
this week?

If you
could go back
and change one thing
about this week, what
would it be?

Write down things you need help with or are worried about. Use this list to help you pray to God each day. Add to this list if new concerns pop up during the week!

Think back on this last week - do you remember any prayers being answered or do you feel like God spoke to you in any way?

TODAYS DATE:

What commercial jingle gets
stuck in your head all the time?

DAILY QUESTION

TO-DO'S, DOODLES, & DREAMS:

Sing a new song to the Lord! Let the whole earth sing to the Lord!

PSALM 96:1

TODAYS DATE:

What was the best gift
you ever received for Christmas
and what was the best
gift you ever gave?

DAILY QUESTION

TO-DO'S, DOODLES, & DREAMS:

Every good action and every perfect gift is from God.
These good gifts come down from the Creator of the sun, moon,
and stars. God does not change like their shifting shadows.

JAMES 1:17

TODAYS DATE:

If you could travel back in time
3 years, what would you tell your
younger self?

DAILY QUESTION

TO-DOS, DOODLES, & DREAMS:

*This means that anyone who belongs to Christ
has become a new person.
The old life is gone; a new life has begun!*

2 CORINTHIANS 5:17

TODAYS DATE:

If there was one thing you could change about yourself, what would it be?

DAILY QUESTION

TO-DO'S, DOODLES, & DREAMS:

Don't you realize that your body is the temple of the Holy Spirit, who lives in you and was given to you by God? You do not belong to yourself, for God bought you with a high price.
So you must honor God with your body.

1 CORINTHIANS 6:19-20

TODAYS DATE:

What's your favorite
thing about yourself?

DAILY QUESTION

TO-DO'S, DOODLES, & DREAMS:

So, as those who have been chosen of God, holy and beloved,
put on a heart of compassion, kindness, humility, gentleness and
patience; bearing with one another, and forgiving each other,
whoever has a complaint against anyone; just as the Lord forgave
you, so also should you. Beyond all these things put on love,
which is the perfect bond of unity.

COLOSSIANS 3:12-14

TODAYS DATE:

If you could cure one
type of disease, which one
would you cure?

DAILY QUESTION

TO-DO'S, DOODLES, & DREAMS:

Confess your sins to each other and pray for each other so that you
may be healed. The earnest prayer of a righteous person
has great power and produces wonderful results.

JAMES 5:16

TODAYS DATE:

When you fall asleep at night, what is the last thing you usually think about?

DAILY QUESTION

TO-DO'S, DOODLES, & DREAMS:

Then Jesus said, "Come to me, all of you who are weary
and carry heavy burdens, and I will give you rest."

MATTHEW 11:28

WEEKLY CHECK-IN

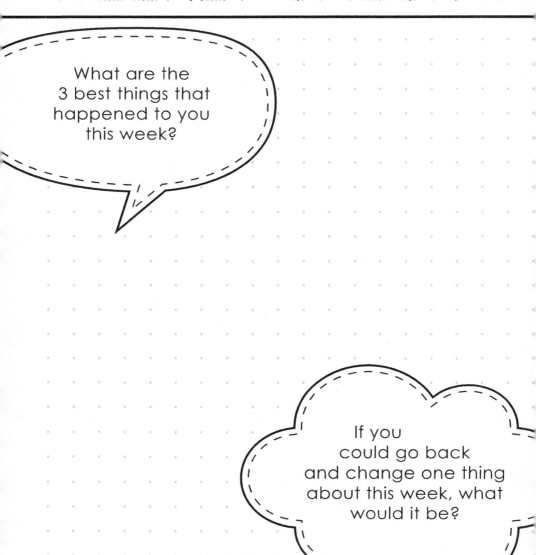

Write down things you need help with or are worried about. Use this list to help you pray to God each day. Add to this list if new concerns pop up during the week!

Think back on this last week - do you remember any prayers being answered or do you feel like God spoke to you in any way?

If you could turn the ocean into a liquid other than water, which one would you pick?

TO-DOS, DOODLES, & DREAMS:

When you go through deep waters, I will be with you.
When you go through rivers of difficulty, you will not drown.

ISAIAH 43:2A

TODAYS DATE:

What do you wish other people knew about you without having to ask?

DAILY QUESTION

TO-DO'S, DOODLES, & DREAMS:

Through his power all things were made—things in heaven and on earth, things seen and unseen, all powers, authorities, lords, and rulers. All things were made through Christ and for Christ.

COLOSSIANS 1:16

What kind of first job
do you want?

TO-DOS, DOODLES, & DREAMS:

Work willingly at whatever you do, as though you were working for the Lord rather than for people.

COLOSSIANS 3:23

TODAYS DATE:

What do you love
about your family?

DAILY QUESTION

TO-DO'S, DOODLES, & DREAMS:

We love because God first loved us.

1 JOHN 4:19

TODAYS DATE:

Do you have any talents?

DAILY QUESTION

TO-DO'S, DOODLES, & DREAMS:

God has given each of you a gift from his great variety
of spiritual gifts. Use them well to serve one another.

1 PETER 4:10

TODAYS DATE:

What three things would you take with you to a deserted island and why?

DAILY QUESTION

TO-DO'S, DOODLES, & DREAMS:

Don't store up treasures here on earth, where moths eat them and rust destroys them, and where thieves break in and steal. Store your treasures in heaven, where moths and rust cannot destroy, and thieves do not break in and steal. Wherever your treasure is, there the desires of your heart will also be.

MATTHEW 6:19-21

TODAYS DATE:

What do you think your life will
be like in 5 years?

DAILY QUESTION

TO-DOS, DOODLES, & DREAMS:

*"For I know the plans I have for you," says the Lord.
"They are plans for good and not for disaster,
to give you a future and a hope."*

JEREMIAH 29:11

WEEKLY CHECK-IN

What are the
3 best things that
happened to you
this week?

If you
could go back
and change one thing
about this week, what
would it be?

Write down things you need help with or are worried about. Use this list to help you pray to God each day. Add to this list if new concerns pop up during the week!

Think back on this last week - do you remember any prayers being answered or do you feel like God spoke to you in any way?

...SO HOW WAS IT?

Over the last
9 weeks, what
did you learn about
yourself that you
didn't know before?

Do you feel like you are closer to God and that he hears your prayers? Is it easier to pray now?

Made in the USA
Las Vegas, NV
17 December 2021

38483618R00083